Mack Wilberg

Carols

*8 carols for mixed voices
by Mack Wilberg*

MUSIC DEPARTMENT

OXFORD
UNIVERSITY PRESS

OXFORD
UNIVERSITY PRESS

198 Madison Avenue, New York, NY, 10016, USA
Great Clarendon Street, Oxford OX2 6DP, England

Oxford University Press is a department of the University of Oxford.
It furthers the University's aim of excellence in research, scholarship,
and education by publishing worldwide

Oxford New York
Auckland Bangkok Buenos Aires Cape Town Chennai
Dar es Salaam Delhi Hong Kong Istanbul Karachi Kolkata
Kuala Lumpur Madrid Melbourne Mexico City Mumbai Nairobi
São Paulo Shanghai Taipei Tokyo Toronto

Oxford is a registered trademark of Oxford University Press

9 10 8

ISBN 978-0-19-387016-1

Music origination by
Barnes Music Engraving Ltd, East Sussex, England

Printed by Halstan and Co. Ltd., England, on acid-free paper

Contents

Index of Alternative Accompaniments and Orchestrations

Scores and orchestral parts are available on hire from the publishers or for sale as indicated below.

Carol to the King
- Piano duet and percussion (snare drum, triangle, bass drum, suspended cymbal, tambourine, chimes, glockenspiel; or snare drum only); (vocal scores with parts available on sale: 978–0–19–386975–2)
- Orchestra: picc.2.2.2.2–4.3.3.1–timp.–3 perc.–strings–harp–optional organ (hire)

Gloria tibi Domine
- Piano duet (978–0–19–386914–1)
- Brass (2 trumpets, horn, 2 trombones, tuba), timpani, percussion, and organ (hire).

How far is it to Bethlehem?
- 2 flutes and harp or piano (vocal scores with parts available on sale: 978–0–19–386425–2)
- 2 flutes, 2 oboes (opt.), strings, and harp or piano (hire)

Infant Holy, Infant lowly
- Strings (hire)

Still, Still, Still
- Piano or organ duet (978–0–19–386927–1)
- Strings (hire)

The Virgin Mary had a baby boy
- Piano duet, shaker, congas, and double bass (vocal scores with parts available on sale 978–0–19–386929–5)
- Orchestra: picc.1.1.1.1–0.3(opt.).3 (opt.).0–steel drums or piano, percussion, and strings (hire)

What shall we give?
- Orchestra: 3.2.2.2–4.0.0.0–harp, and strings (hire)

Please contact the publishers for a full catalogue of Oxford music by Mack Wilberg.

Available Recordings

Carol to the King

• DVD 'Christmas with the Mormon Tabernacle Choir and Orchestra at Temple Square: Volume 2' (available at www.mormontabernaclechoir.org)

Gloria tibi Domine
Lullee, Lullai, Lullo, Lullabye (SATB and organ)

• CD 'Cantate Hodie: Sing Forth this Day' (Clarion, CLR 903 CD)

How far is it to Bethlehem?
What shall we give?

• CD 'A Mormon Tabernacle Choir Christmas' (available at
      www.mormontabernaclechoir.org)

Infant Holy, Infant Lowly
Still, Still, Still
The Virgin Mary had a baby boy

• CD 'Sing, Choirs of Angels' available at www.mormontabernaclechoir.org)
• CD 'Simple Gifts' by Bryn Terfel (Deutsche Grammophon B0004772-02)

Acknowledgements

The publishers gratefully acknowledge the help of Ralph Woodward in preparing some of the single piano accompaniments.

for the Mormon Tabernacle Choir, Craig Jessop, Music Director

Carol to the King

(A Christmas Processional)

Jim Christian

French Carol
arr. MACK WILBERG

Lyrics: Can you hear the dis - tant mu - sic Sound-ing from the pipe and horn,

* Bass part may also be sung by second tenors here.

Bear-ing news of joy and glad-ness "Christ, the King of heav'n is born."

An-gels, too, re - sound the an-them To the child-ren of the earth,

Call-ing all to hear the ti-dings Of the bless-ed Sav-ior's birth,

Hear them sing, "Ta-ra-ra, ta-ra-rè-re, Li - tam-

-pon, la-dé-ri-tam-pon," the fife and an-gel voi-ces ring._____

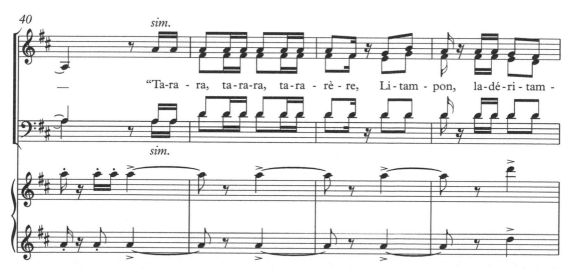

sim.

"Ta-ra-ra, ta-ra-ra, ta-ra-rè-re, Li-tam-pon, la-dé-ri-tam-

sim.

4

-pon," they all re - joice with songs they sing to bring the world a new-born

King!

S.
A.

Feel the mu - sic stir your sen - ses Like a might - y trum - pet call,

TENORS

T.

56

Wak - en - ing the world from slum - ber Call - ing out to one and all,

From the vil - lage, from the coun - try Let us join the ho - ly throng,

As we hast - en to the man - ger That we, too, may join the song.

As we sing, "Ta-ra-ra, ta-ra - rè - re, Li - tam - pon, la-dé-ri - tam -

-pon," the fife and an-gel voi-ces ring._____ "Ta-ra -

-ra, ta-ra-ra, ta-ra - rè - re, Li - tam - pon, la-dé-ri - tam - pon," we all re -

- joice with songs they sing to bring the world a new - born

King!

En - ter now the ho - ly sta - ble To be - hold the bless - ed sight,

This is Christ, the Lord, the Sav - ior, Pure and filled with ho - ly light,

Tune your heart to hear His mu - sic, Feel the glo - ry of His love,

134

Let us wor-ship and a-dore Him, Won-drous Child of God a-bove.

138

ff

Raise your voice, "Ta-ra-ra, ta-ra - rè - re, Li-tam - pon, la-dé-ri-tam -

ff

142

-pon," the fife and an-gel voi-ces ring._____ "Ta-ra -

a new - born King,_____

a new - born King!_____

Commissioned by the Barlow Endowment for Music Composition at Brigham Young University
for the Bach Choir of Pittsburgh and Pittsburgh Symphony Brass, Brady Allred, Conductor

Gloria tibi Domine

15th-cent. English carol

MACK WILBERG

Glo - ri - a ti - bi Do - mi - ne, glo - ri - a ti - bi Do - mi - ne,
(Glory be to Thee, Lord, who are born of a virgin)

17

glo-ri-a ti – bi Do – mi-ne Qui na – tus es___ de vir – gi – ne.

21 *(upper voices equally divided a3)*

Glo-ri-a ti – bi Do – mi-ne, glo-ri-a ti – bi Do – mi-ne,

25

S.
A.

glo-ri-a ti – bi Do – mi-ne Qui na – tus es___ de

T.
B.

T./B.   *unis.* **mf**

A

16

glo-ri-a ti - bi Do - mi-ne Qui na - tus es___ de vir - gi-ne.

Glo-ri-a ti - bi Do - mi-ne, glo-ri-a ti - bi Do - mi-ne,

glo-ri-a ti - bi Do - mi-ne Qui na - tus es___ de vir - gi-ne.

-sus that is so full__ of might, Je - sus that is so full__ of might, Y-

-bore he was a - bout__ mid-night The an - gels sung with all here might,
(their)

Je - sus is that chil - de's name, Je - sus is that chil - de's name,

kings there came with here_ pre-sence, three kings there came with here_ pre-sence, Of
(their)

myrre and gold and frank-en-sence As clerk-es sing_ in here se-quence.

24

Set we down up - on___ our knee, Now set we down up - on___ our knee, And

pray that child that is___ so free, And with good heart___ now sing we:

Glo-ri-a ti - bi Do - mi-ne, glo-ri-a ti - bi Do - mi-ne,

136

glo-ri-a ti - bi Do - mi-ne Qui na - tus es___ de vir - gi-ne.

140

Glo-ri-a ti - bi Do - mi-ne, glo-ri-a ti - bi Do - mi-ne,

144

glo-ri-a ti - bi Do - mi-ne Qui na - tus es, qui

148

na - tus es,　　　　qui　na - tus es,　qui　na - tus es,　qui

152

na - tus es＿ de　vir - gi - ne.

157

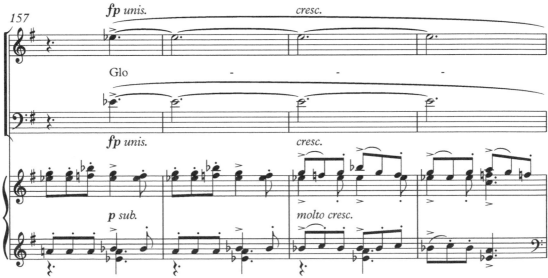

fp unis.　　　　　　　　*cresc.*

Glo　—　　—　　—

fp unis.　　　　　　　*cresc.*

p sub.　　　　　*molto cresc.*

for the Mormon Tabernacle Choir, Craig Jessop, Music Director

How far is it to Bethlehem?

Frances Chesterton

English Carol
arr. MACK WILBERG

The words of Frances Chesterton are set to music and reproduced by permission of A. P. Watt Limited on behalf of The Royal Literary Fund.

star? Can we see the lit - tle child, is he with -

- in? If___ we lift the wood - en latch, may we go

in?

* stagger breathing

ti - ny hand will He a - wake? Will He know we've come so far

just for his sake?

cresc.

32

* stagger breathing

brought. For all wea-ry child-ren Ma-ry must weep,

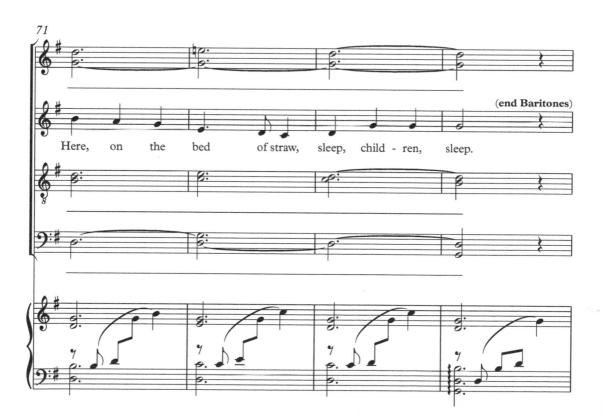

(end Baritones)

Here, on the bed of straw, sleep, child-ren, sleep.

34

God in his mo - ther's arms; Babes in the byre

Sleep, as they sleep who find Their heart's de - sire.

rit.   Meno mosso

poco rit.   a tempo   rit.

for the Mormon Tabernacle Choir, Craig Jessop, Music Director

Infant Holy, Infant lowly

W żłobie leży
trans. Edith M. G. Reed (1885–1933)*

Polish Carol
arr. MACK WILBERG

* First published in *Music and Youth* (Vol. 1, no. 12, December 1921)

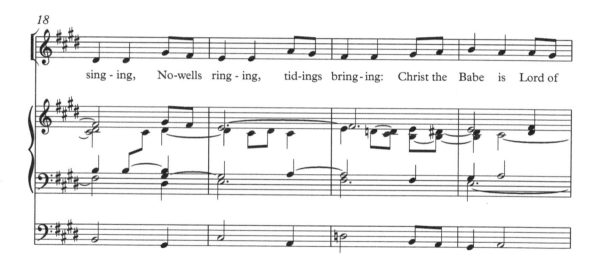

Flocks were sleep - ing, shep-herds keep - ing Vi - gil

till the morn-ing new_____ Saw the glo - ry, heard the sto - ry, Tid-ings

of a gos-pel true.__ Thus re - joic - ing, free from sor - row, Prais-es

voic - ing, greet the mor - row: Christ the Babe was born for you.__

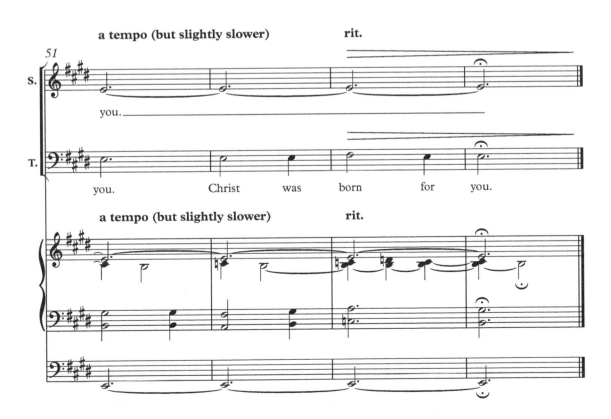

*Commissioned by the Barlow Endowment for Music Composition at Brigham Young University
for the Bach Choir of Pittsburgh and Pittsburgh Brass; Brady Allred, Conductor*

Lullee, lullai, lullo, lullabye

(O who will come and listen this night?)

David Warner

MACK WILBERG

* Rhyme with "lullabye"

a tempo

Lul - lee, lul - lai, The shep - herds do

poco rit.

sigh. Lul - lee, lul - lai, lul - lo, lul - la - bye.

a tempo
SOPRANO (SOLO or SEMI-CHORUS)

O who will come to His moth - er so mild Who knows the

Man to Ped. 8'
(*double pedalling optional*)

path of her in - no-cent Child that leads to where none

44

Man. to Ped. 8' & soft 8'
(*double pedalling optional*)

46

for the Mormon Tabernacle Choir, Craig Jessop, Music Director

Still, still, still

David Warner

Austrian Carol
arr. MACK WILBERG

Ma - ry,_ breath-less, draws Him, weep-ing, To her heart made pure for_ keep-ing.

Still,_ still,_ still, His_ bright eyes_ soft - ly_ close._

S./A. *p unis. sempre*

Sing,_ sing,_ sing, He_

Sleep, sleep, O sleep._____ He breathes a sigh_____

Sleep,_ sleep,_ sleep,_ He_ breathes a____ ten - der_ sigh, For

For soon He'll wake from slum-ber, Bring-ing life and end - less won-der,

soon He'll wake the world from slum-ber, Bring-ing_ life and end - less won-der,

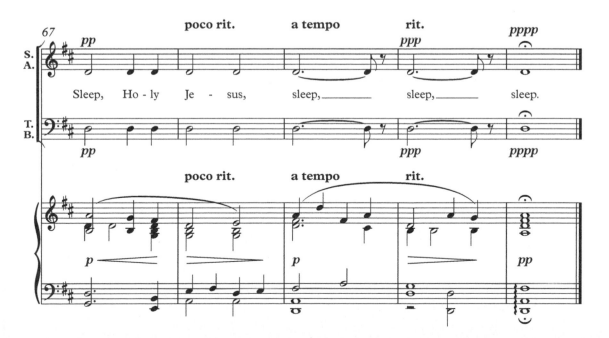

The Virgin Mary had a baby boy

Trad. West Indian Carol
arr. MACK WILBERG

Calypso style (♩ = *c*.120–6)

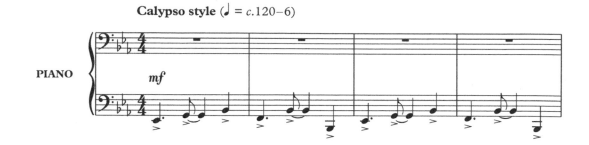

He come from the glo - ry, He come from the

glo - ri - ous King - dom.

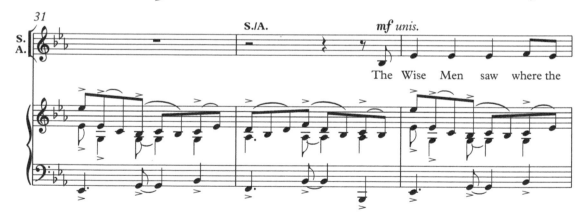

S./A.   *mf unis.*

The Wise Men saw where the

ba-by was born, the Wise Men saw where the ba-by was born, the

Wise Men saw where the ba-by was born, And they said that his name was

Je - sus. He come from the glo - ry,

He come from the glo-ri-ous King - dom, He come from the

glo - ry, He come from the glo-ri-ous King - dom.

Oh, yes, be-lie-ver, Oh,
yes, be-lie-ver, He come from the glo - ry,
He come_ from the glo-ri - ous King - dom,

74

ba-by was born, the an - gels sang when the ba-by was born, the

77

an - gels sang when the ba-by was born, and they said that his name was

80   *unis.*

Je - sus.   He come from the glo - ry,

unis.

glo - ri - ous King - dom, glo - ri - ous, glo - ri - ous,

Yes,_____ He come from the

glo - ri - ous King - dom, glo - ri - ous King - dom,

for the Mormon Tabernacle Choir, Craig Jessop, Music Director

What shall we give?

David Warner

Catalonian Carol
arr. MACK WILBERG

tam, pa-tan, tan - tam; tam, pa-tan, tam, pa-tan, tam, pa-tan-tam;

tam, pa-tan, tam, pa-tan, tam, pa-tan, tan - tam; tam, pa-tan, tam, pa-tan,

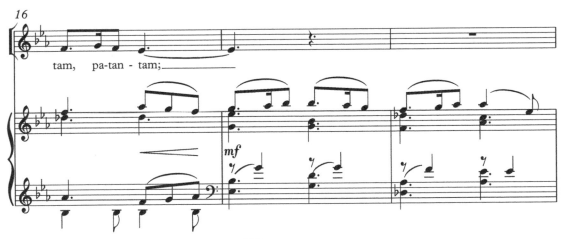

tam, pa-tan - tam;

TENOR

What shall we give to the Boy in the tem - ple? What shall we of - fer the

Man by the sea? Palms at His feet and ho - san - nas up - ris - ing,

are these for Him who will car - ry the tree? Tam, pa-tan, tam, pa-tan,

What shall we give to the

Lamb who was of - fered, ris - ing the third day and shed - ding His Love?_____

Tears for His mer - cy we'll weep at the man - ger; bath - ing the In - fant come

down from a - bove. Tam, pa-tan, tam, pa-tan, tam, pa-tan, tan - tam;

tam, pa-tan, tam, pa-tan, tam, pa-tan-tam; tam, pa-tan, tam, pa-tan,

tam, pa-tan, tan - tam; tam, pa-tan, tam, pa-tan, tam, pa-tan-tam;

* stagger breathing

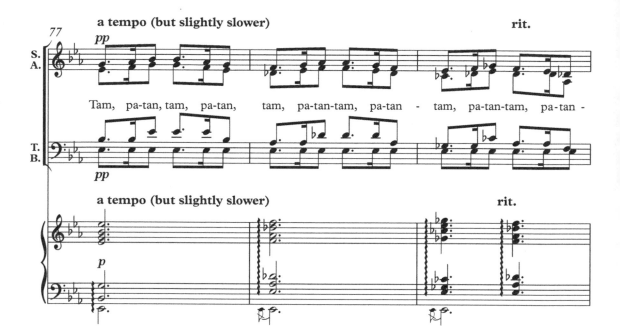

Tam, pa-tan, tam, pa-tan, tam, pa-tan-tam, pa-tan - tam, pa-tan-tam, pa-tan -

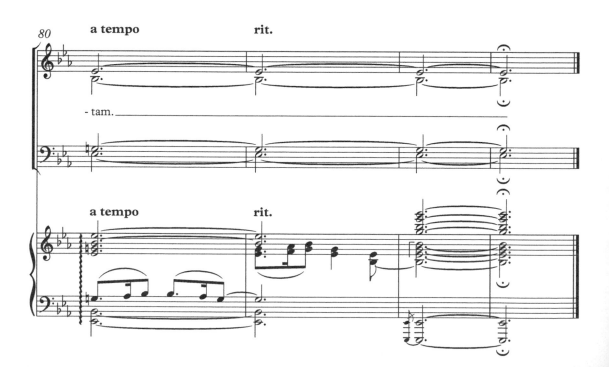

- tam.